Commun

The Ultimate Guide for Communal Living And What You Need to Know

presentation of the information is without contract or any type of guarantee assurance.

The trademarks that are used are without any consent, and the publication of the trademark is without permission or backing by the trademark owner. All trademarks and brands within this book are for clarifying purposes only and are the owned by the owners themselves, not affiliated with this document.

Table Of Contents

Introduction

The pages in this book were developed through years of experiences that I have gone through, as well as what has proven to work for others that I have talked to and have researched. This short book is for people who are interested in learning more about how to proceed with communal living and are not sure where to start or what information to rely on.

After experiencing many different types of living arrangements throughout my life and learning to adapt to them, I decided that I wanted to write a short, detailed book to help other people who are in a similar situation as I was. I also wanted to help people understand how to view communal living from a historical viewpoint and how to proceed despite the challenges they will face.

Intentional living and communal life is gaining more acceptance in the sociological perspective. Even governments now encourage communal living. This is so because the system enhances moral uprightness, ecological awareness, and economic benefits. In the latter aspect, it gives advantages to the group members in particular, and the state or government, both from an individual perspective and from the macro viewpoint. Within these rational considerations, communal life must be seriously considered as an alternative lifestyle.

However, sometimes communal living arrangements are misunderstood from the public eye. Some people believe that these arrangements are only for "hippies" or people who are lazy. This is far from the truth. People from all demographics, poor and rich, from all different backgrounds, are engaging in these types of living arrangements because of the many advantages it provides.

I am not going to tell you what you should do while living in a communal environment as that goes directly against the point of living in such a way. Commune life should be determined by the people who are directly involved with it. The philosophical ideals and monetary policies are up to those individuals, which is what makes it so beautiful.

I recommend that you take notes while you are reading this book as it will ensure that you get the most out of the information in here. I want you to feel you have made a purchase that is worth your money and you can also look over the notes of this book even after you've finished reading it. The notes will help you to pinpoint exactly what you need to implement and by writing things down, you will be able to recall specifics when certain situations arise.

Lastly, remember that everything in this book has been compiled through research, my own experiences, as well as the experiences of others, so feel free to question what you have read in this book. I encourage you to do your own research on the things that you want to look deeper into. The more you understand about the obstacles that you will deal with in a communal living arrangement, the more educated your decision-making process will be when it comes to taking action or giving advice to others.

Chapter 1:

Understanding Communal Living

The History and Origins of Communal Living

Communal living refers to a planned community where people live together and share common interests, resources, properties, and possessions. In certain instances, they also pool their work, or industry, and their income.

For the non-economic concerns, many communal units decide important factors by consensus among members, and there is no definite structure in the organizational hierarchy. Communal living therefore hinges more on the logic and philosophy regarding doing what is best for everyone. Caring for the environment and maintaining ecological balance have also become important concerns in communal life during recent times.

From the macro viewpoint, communal living is actually a cooperative existence in which the objective is to give each member adequate and healthy living space, while also maintaining that no individual becomes richer and more influential than the others in the community.

Communes, particularly in the United States, are generally geared toward a pragmatic way of life and financial solvency. From the political perspective, communal living is perceived to be the historical proponent of communism. Within the sociological and economic concepts, communal living encourages a social order where there is no class, no monopoly of monetary advantage, and where the members are not beholden to leaders, except to keep the community peaceful and orderly.

The abundance of goods is made available for access to the members in a distribution arrangement that is based on need and social responsibility. It must be emphasized that the second basis is social responsibility and not social class or status. As a matter of fact, one core principle of commune living is the presumption of a classless clustering.

Commune living finds its origin in the theory of life in utopia, which means "no place", as if to imply that classification of persons has no place in commune living.

In the order of epochs, the first proposition of a utopian existence is found in the Republic, the most well-known work of Plato, which deals with socio-economic policy and philosophy. Here, Plato must have realized the need to neutralize the inequities, and possibly the injustice, brought about by the dominance of royalties.

In it, Plato proposes that citizens be rigidly categorized into several class structures. These socio-economic classifications were the gold, silver, bronze and iron of society. The golden class pertained to the benevolent oligarchs or royal philosophers. The wise thinking of these monarchs would purportedly wipe out poverty and the deprivation of basic human needs.

Although the minute details of the manner by which to do it was not unequivocal, the supposition was that it would be through the fair distribution of resources among the subjects. The rulers would undergo a fifty year educational discipline. There would be few laws and there would be no lawyers. Rarely would citizens be sent to wars or battles. Instead, mercenaries would be hired, when needed, under dangerous circumstances in a long-range scheme that in the end, only people of peace would remain to exist, vanishing warriors and combatants.

In essence, as early as before the time of Christ, Plato had already thought of a self-sufficient society free of hunger and need, where there was stability in peace and where legal issues were made wanting as much as could be in order to generally avoid conflict, indifference, and aloofness between and amongst individuals. The latter characteristic explains why Plato's proposition for a fifty year royal mentoring specifically excludes lawyers.

Intentional communities in the form of communal living have been established and developed in more than many locations worldwide in the hope that a perfect lifestyle is made over time. Despite all the efforts toward that end, many attempts have failed. There are a few, however, which have survived and have shown significant proof of progress. One is the Twelve Tribes Communities, which was started in the United States and has been branching out into many locations around the globe. It is true that there are allegations of improprieties but, as a whole, this communal living system has sustained well in its existence. Some of the accusations may be exceptions or remote instances.

Types of Commune Systems

There are many types of communal living structures.

Communal living founded on ecological considerations define ways and means by which societies recognize the importance of caring for nature. The movers of this type of communal living advance the perception that the modern lifestyle of the West has destroyed, and continues to destroy, the natural environment.

Corollary to that, it is propositioned that better living ways are the traditional ones, which were observed before the advent of industrialization and which are more prudently harmonious with nature and in accordance with sustainability.

In the nineteen sixties, communes in the United States started and flourished in the crusade to enhance the way of life. Life in togetherness inside and among communities was being dreamt to be one that was peaceful and hunger free, where every human was treated equally.

There were movements to encourage going back to the farmlands. Hippies were giving inspiration to those in the urbanities to try living in peace and amity in the rural areas in far flung villages and in other indigenous places, in hopes to establish self-governance and communal lives under novel but dynamic, and though sometimes radical, concepts.

Religious or faith precepts were later on injected into the movement for communal living. Intra-religious and inter-religious efforts were focused on the feasibility of leaders of religions to set aside their conflicting ideas of faith, or of politics, and to unite as one in order to promote peace, harmony, and understanding in the whole world. These attempts for a good cause were made both within and among religious orders. In effect, the informal but widespread movements were actually geared toward promoting the social order of communal living, even in the religious landscape.

Another example of commune living is the kibbutz structure. It is a very successful one. This system of collective community in Israel is actually a classic demonstration that commune living can be stable and prosperous. Initially, the kibbutz was established for agricultural purposes. However, through the passage of time, it has evolved into a more expanded role.

Presently, farming is already complemented by industrial activities and high technology ventures. Kibbutzim (the plural for kibbutz) initially were utopian communities governed by Zionist and socialist theories. The first kibbutz came into being in the year 1909. Kibbutzim have achieved staggering financial successes, with its 2010 total output amounting to around eight billion United States dollars (US$8,000,000,000). It has also branched out into tourism. Additionally, the cooperative spirit in the kibbutz mechanics have helped Israel in its war efforts and in its defense initiatives.

From the start, the kibbutz movement faced many trials and challenges. First off, the founders were migrants to Palestine. Their only aim then was to become farmers, individually tending to the fields in peace, quiet, and happiness and to live in moral contentment.

In the course of their survival occupation, they thought of a better way to uplift their lives. They decided for group settlements in order to parry the harshness and difficulties of the prevailing negative factors. The general environment was not conducive to good farming as well as convenient living. On one side, the Galilee was marshy, the hills along the Judea were rocky, while the south side was a desert.

What made matters so tough was the lack of experience on the part of the new settlers in agricultural workmanship. Furthermore, the surroundings were unsanitary, resulting in health conditions being poor. Malaria, cholera, and typhus proliferated while many uncivilized intruders would come to assault and ransack the cultivated areas and occupied these for their own settlement.

Irrigation canals were sabotaged and crops were burned. To remedy all of these contrasts and backlashes, the only way was to unite and to work and live collectively. One important factor was that a farming venture needed intensive capital and the collective financial and material resources of the kibbutz founders played a very significant role.

Among all genders and age categories, the idea of living in commune is now gaining ground. Female baby boomers, for instance, are deciding to age with the support of friends from, or within, their own ranks. Supposedly more empowered than the previous generations of adult females, they claim to be more financially sound and prepared, more sophisticated and physically healthier than their predecessors.

Additionally, these new groups of women choose to remain active as they age. They have resolved to continue moving on with life in fun camaraderie, good humor, and a keen desire to learn and understand. Together with these positive outlooks, they seek the support of their women friends who adopt the same healthy lifestyle and clean living. Also included in the communal living agenda of these women are a myriad of activities, such as the organic cultivation of their own gardens where they grow healthy food, as well as other environmentally friendly endeavors.

Home sharing programs, a communal living concept, have also trended among these women baby boomers. In the year 2010, about four hundred eighty thousand of these aged ladies lived with at least one female companion not related to them. As a matter of fact, since the decline of the economy, these numbers have been rising steadily. Areas of concentration are on the East and West Coasts, and they appear to be even more common in the United States than in Europe.

While home sharing also prevails among men, the percentage is greater in women. This is explained by the fact that men usually re-marry quicker after the passing of the spouse, or after being separated and/or divorced. Hence, males usually do not need much help from outside of the domestic home.

Another explanation is that women also live longer than men. Also, even in today's rapidly changing political and workforce structure, men are still usually higher earners than their female counterparts. Some men feel more of a hit to the ego if they are not able to provide for their own private living space. Meanwhile, women tend to not be as rigid with that ideal. Furthermore, women are generally more bonded amongst themselves in a special way, more likely to develop "sisterhood".

Co-homed women enjoy their happy moments in talks over coffee or some other beverage, in laughter while watching movies together or while having their meals. Sometimes, confiding or pouring out certain grievances are included in the companionships.

The atmosphere in co-home arrangements is set in such a way that residents have their own individual private living areas. However, they tend to share certain spaces, such as the receiving room. They also engage in some tasks in common such as cooking and marketing. The co-home movement began in Denmark and spread to the United States. As a matter of fact, there are model projects set up in Colorado and other locations. Three co-home programs are currently being schemed out in the Nashville, Tennessee area.

While it is inspiring to hear stories of commune living as shown by the new co-home culture, there are practical and pragmatic concerns which must be addressed first. In establishing these communities, as in other similar systems, the health and safety of the participating adults have to be assured. Next, care in case of accident or medical urgencies must be anticipated. Lastly, the financial capabilities, limitations, and reservations of these people should be assessed and evaluated, both as individuals and as a whole.

The latter consideration, particularly, becomes more important because money is always a serious issue for those who now realize that, after years of marriage, they have become single or widowed. It has to be taken into account that baby boomers, maybe due to their age and insecurity or uncertainty, demand more comfort than just what nature can provide for them.

Yes, they assert that they are happy and healthy. They claim that they are active and wish to enjoy themselves as they age. Yet, they also want to go on leisurely trips. They want to go to the movies with neighbors or housemates, cook their own meals or share gardening activities. Therefore, aside from receiving or enjoying basic items of attention, they themselves also wish to feel that they contribute to the communities. While they say they are strong individuals, they also opt, as they become older, to live a life in a way that they want - a lifestyle of design.

Hence, in summing it up, it is easy to set up co-home structures for communal living among young adults or aging men and women belonging to the baby boom generation. However, problems may possibly arise concerning logistics and resources. Unless all the purported participants are, or have been, fully covered by insurance for retirement and healthcare provisions, certain predicaments might be encountered by the managing or monitoring agencies.

While support groups will be of great help, there are no blueprinted assurances to respond to the whole caboodle. Further studies, recommendations, and legislative actions, especially for budget purposes, may be required to institutionalize this type of communal living and to make it work even more effectively.

Chapter 2:

Inspirations And Movers

There are internet based entities which give information on communal living systems and communities. One based in London declares itself to be a non-profit organization. It claims that one of its aims is to bring the structure of communal living in the United Kingdom to the awareness of a more expanded population.

In line with that objective, it has produced several publications on commune life information since 1989. Some are in hard copy or paper versions and others are electronically generated on its website. Aside from articles on commune life systems, it also publishes directories. It has also conducted interviews on the theme of communal living, one of which was on co-home arrangements within the United Kingdom.

If one therefore wishes to find a prospective home or group for communal living in the United Kingdom, it might be worth a try going to its website for further information and details. There are also guides and steps if one intends to make a visit to a certain community or to a number of these communities. If you are interested, the communities listed in the directories may be physically visited or contacted for information about joining.

As a matter of course, each community has its set of disciplines, requirements, and systems of organization and operations. There is therefore a need to personally know all of these upon entering. Since contributions to the chosen communities can vary, one has to anticipate and/or prepare for monetary requirements.

Another group, with its main headquarters based in the state of Missouri in the United States, also caters to those who need, or wish to have, information on communes and intentional communities, among others. Its services also cover eco-villages, cooperatives, land trusts, and co-home arrangements.

In the nineteen sixties, young people who seemed to have rejected societal standards because of the rebellious spirit in them, or because of any opposing view to the more acceptable social order, stopped schooling or other formal disciplines and left for the country atmosphere. There, they tried experimenting the utopian way of life.

Beyond negative urban cultures and suburban similarities, they started building lives in a new environment with novel or modified political objectives and sociological concepts. They went into full time community service, including engagement in organic farming and other ecological friendly efforts.

Surviving simply in life with their peers, they have grouped themselves in clusters of artists, philosophical and practical idealists, musicians, poets, and writers. They have also developed themselves into communities dedicated to the structuring of families in redefined ways and manners.

They made adjustments between pleasure and work and in the role of their commune style of living in the global backdrops. The levels of success are in varying forms though. Some men, together with some women, strived to equate political and personal liberties with individual accountabilities and committed undertakings. They tapped themselves of their inherent potential and, in the process, have developed skills and expertise in agriculture and construction, which are needed by the communities they have established, according to the desired maintenance and sustainability.

Communal living is making sense in the present global stage because of the general frustration among those who do not belong to the comfort levels in the economic ladder. The common perception, be it right or wrong, that the rich become richer and the poor become poorer drives people away from the realities of materialism. They try to find refuge or escape in other avenues. They try to source out for some options or alternatives to a seemingly no-win situation.

In the development and construction industry alone, the feeling of desperation over new macro and expensive concepts in infrastructure is already overwhelming. Land and buildings are developed for gated communities, according to the primary consideration of domestic security and the alleged secondary factor of profit-making.

Middle income earners and above, who are typically American whites, are the usual entrants to, and occupants in, these new edifices. These new residents and constituents put up such justifications for avoiding the hazards posed by the counter-culture populace in these parts of the city, supposedly allotted to the marginalized citizens.

They also give the excuse of preserving the value of their properties, which is why the tough and formidable structural defense has to be literally put in place. Incidentally, those earning less outnumber those who can afford this lifestyle.

Consciously or subconsciously, the observant low class elements frown upon these novice notions in establishing communities in metropolitan cities.

These trends aggravate the already pernicious and persistent discrimination. They also deepen the insecurity in the feelings of those in the bottom lines of the society. The most that the underprivileged can do is to conform to reality, albeit in pretense or hypocrisy. Oftentimes, the lands for current developments belong to, and are managed by, corporations in the private sector.

The government, both on the federal and state level, no longer have any control of these real properties except maybe for some petty and routine regulations. The second class citizens therefore can do close to nothing. To console and render relief to themselves of their sadness and helplessness, they feel the need to deviate or divert.

They may put up the argument that the air in the country farm is fresh and there is no good reason not going there, living in commune with their equals, and adopting a new life of peace and quiet. If not that, they will advance the thinking that now is the moment to reciprocate to the goodness of nature.

It is now the time to gather friends or family, organize groups or teams to embark into commune living for the sake of ecology, and do things or cause to do things in a common effort that will help the environment recover from human damage, most notably coming from the capitalist polluters.

If still it is not that, they will try going into co-home arrangements with their peers. In this set-up, they will live in one building for abode, but with individual private living spaces, pool portions of their earnings for common expenditures in order to save or economize, share in practical or pragmatic places for common undertakings like, say, eating meals in one building, and doing most of the regular tasks in common efforts by using common tools, machineries, instruments, and equipment.

Co-housing communities or co-home arrangements govern themselves via consensus among members, a characteristic which is actually almost uniform in any intentional community. Also, as is again usual in intentional communities, there are no formal organization mandates or specifics. Instead, meetings to gather consensus, committee work and hours in voluntary services, contribute to the democratic process. In one co-home cluster, committees are led by individual members, respectively, for planning, consensus procedures, kitchen maintenance, pet issues, organic gardening, and conflict resolutions.

Member residents ordinarily agree to render a number of hours to serve the community on a weekly basis, preparing meals, waste composting, tending the gardens, and assisting tours. Since members normally have outside employment, they remit to the community coffers a regular or fixed fee for maintenance and food.

As far as ecology villages undertaken as a commune, these started to come into existence around two decades ago. Their main features are housing structures designed for co-housing clusters. They are established as communities in rural and quasi-rural locations and are built on usually big parcels of lots. With the mission and goals aimed at living in harmony, they adopt sustainable concepts for survival within an ecosystem structure compatible to the locality.

Owing to the fact that houses are clustered in an ecology village, most of its land is used for the restoration of prairies or forests, and for small organic farming. Residential buildings incorporate ecological friendly fixtures including solar and wind energy, if available. Some model ecology villages serve as educational or training centers for environmental studies. Due to their focus on, and promotion of, communal living and education, ecology villages enjoy certain tax exemptions from the United States government.

All of these accounts evidently manifest the advent of communal living as the new alternative in the sociological structure of countries and nations.

Chapter 3:

The Future of Communal Living

As mentioned, there are plenty of concerns that have encouraged people to go into communal living structures. One is for the sake of helping the environment, as demonstrated by the advent of ecology villages and their steady rise in number.

The second is economic consideration, as life in commune is usually prudent. Besides, the pooling of resources and spending as one, results in an economy of scale. Hence, substantial savings accruing to each individual member is an added benefit. This is particularly true in co-housing communities or co-home arrangements.

Another reason addresses the more personal concerns, such as loneliness in retirement, protection and safety, as in the case of women employees who form a group for a co-home structure in order to pool their resources or earnings. Some also do this in order to provide sufficient security and safety for themselves and the satisfaction of faith orientations, especially the counter-cultures who have made amends for their lives. They find a haven in the countryside conducive to the supposed healing and cleansing of their souls.

Also, refugees who flee their war torn hometowns or those who evade cruel punishments, or even those who escape mass executions have increased in great numbers. Once in the host country, they have no other choice but to settle under a commune system so that they will not become a burden to the territory which has welcomed them.

In summation, it is expected that communal living will continue to flourish and multiply and it is probable that the commune system might later on become more standard in large, populated   cities.

Similar propositions

There have been other propositions which are somewhat sophisticated and, as a matter of course, expensive. One is the concept of communities in the middle of oceans, also referred to as seasteading. For the extremely wealthy, a village in the middle of the high seas, which cannot be covered by any jurisdiction from any country, can be designed for a group of individuals looking for a change in political and financial structure.

A hundred or so of them can collectively conceptualize and implement such an idea, and this is actually already gaining momentum... Just go search "seasteading" on Google. For sure, the seasteading life will be free of outside pollution, red tape corruption, and the other negative aspects present and prevalent in mainland living. It may be a very expensive and ambitious undertaking.

However, for as long as it is possible with sufficient and adequate financial resources, a project like that can be realized by the world's rich. At any rate, with the pooling of funds of these very privileged few, the cost per person basis may be verily affordable for each individual. Hence, luxurious commune living in the middle of the Pacific Ocean or in the midst of the Atlantic vastness might no longer be an impossible dream.

Conclusion

I worked hard on creating the best guide for communal living that I could. After finally overcoming many obstacles from a variety of different living arrangements, I wanted to give back to others who were curious about this type of life. These are all the strategies and information that has worked for me, as well as others that I have talked to and researched. I guarantee if you stay consistent they will work for you as well. Be optimistic about your current situation and make small progress each day!

Plus, a little addition to your knowledge base does not hurt, right? It's good to know about these things because the world is slowly starting to become more integrated in the big cities, especially within the United States.

Finally, if you learned something from this book, please take the time to share your thoughts by sending me a message or even posting a review to Amazon.

Thank you and good luck on your journey!

Printed in Great Britain
by Amazon